The following photographs are property of Aisling photography and Kevin Traynor

Aisling Photography Publishing

Belfast

www.aislingphotographyni.co.uk

Kevin Traynor asserts the moral right to be identified as the author of this work.
Nationalist Murals of Northern Ireland 2

ISBN   978-1-4092-7348-6

All rights reserved. No part of this publication may be reproduced, stored in a retrieval system, or transmitted, in any form or by any means, electronic, mechanical, photocopying, recording or otherwise, without the prior permission of the publishers.

IRISH REPUBLICAN MURALS

PHOTOGRAPHS BY KEVIN TRAYNOR

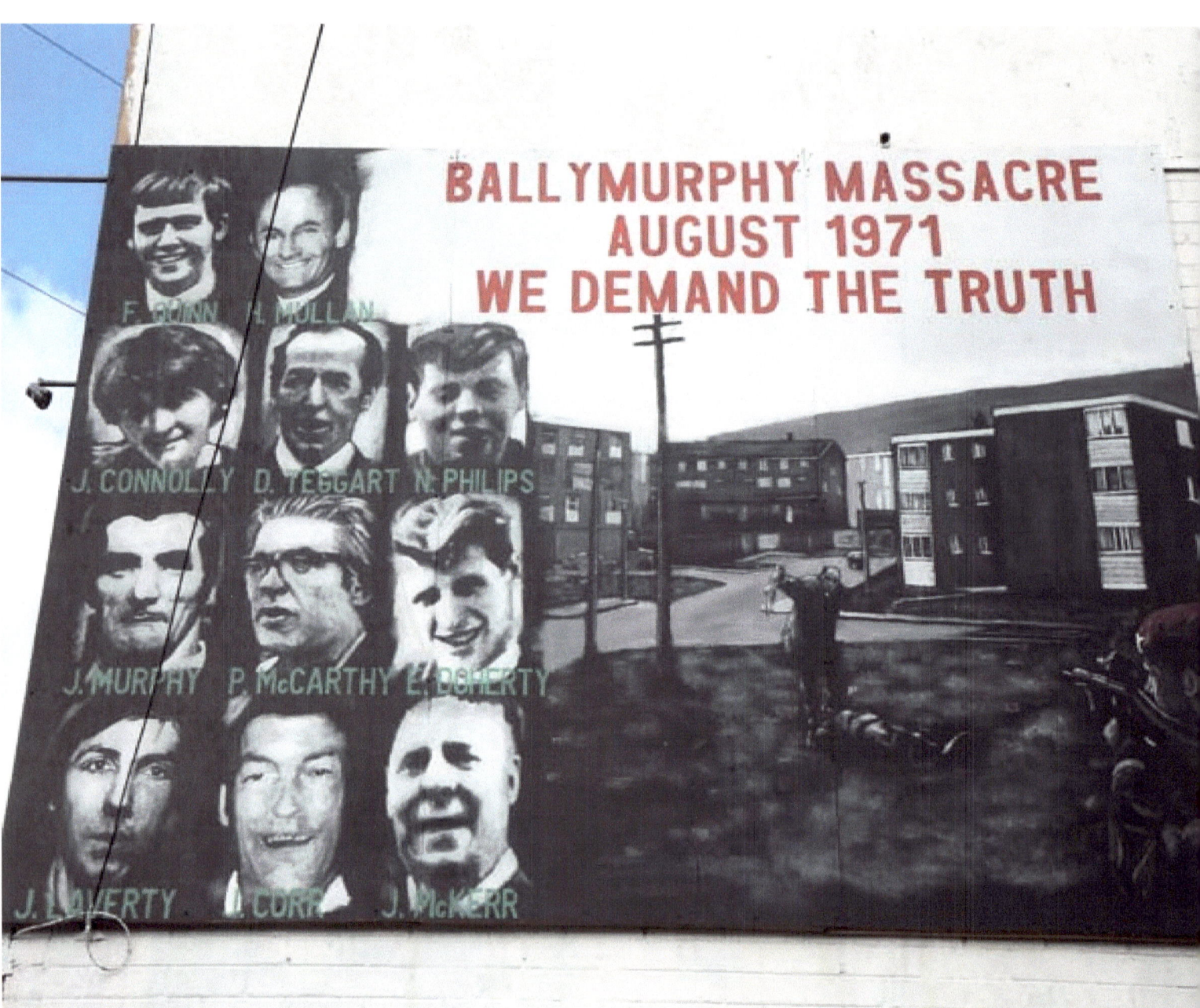

BOMBAY STREET NEVER AGAIN!

Dedicated to the Memory of Fiann Gerald Mc Auley

No Welcome 4
RIR/UDR
MURDERERS
www.osf.ie

Vol. Jake McGerrigan

Vol. Peadar McEloanna

Fuair Siad Bás
Ar Son
Saoirse
na
hÉireann

Vol. Tony Hughes

Vol. Gerard Mallon

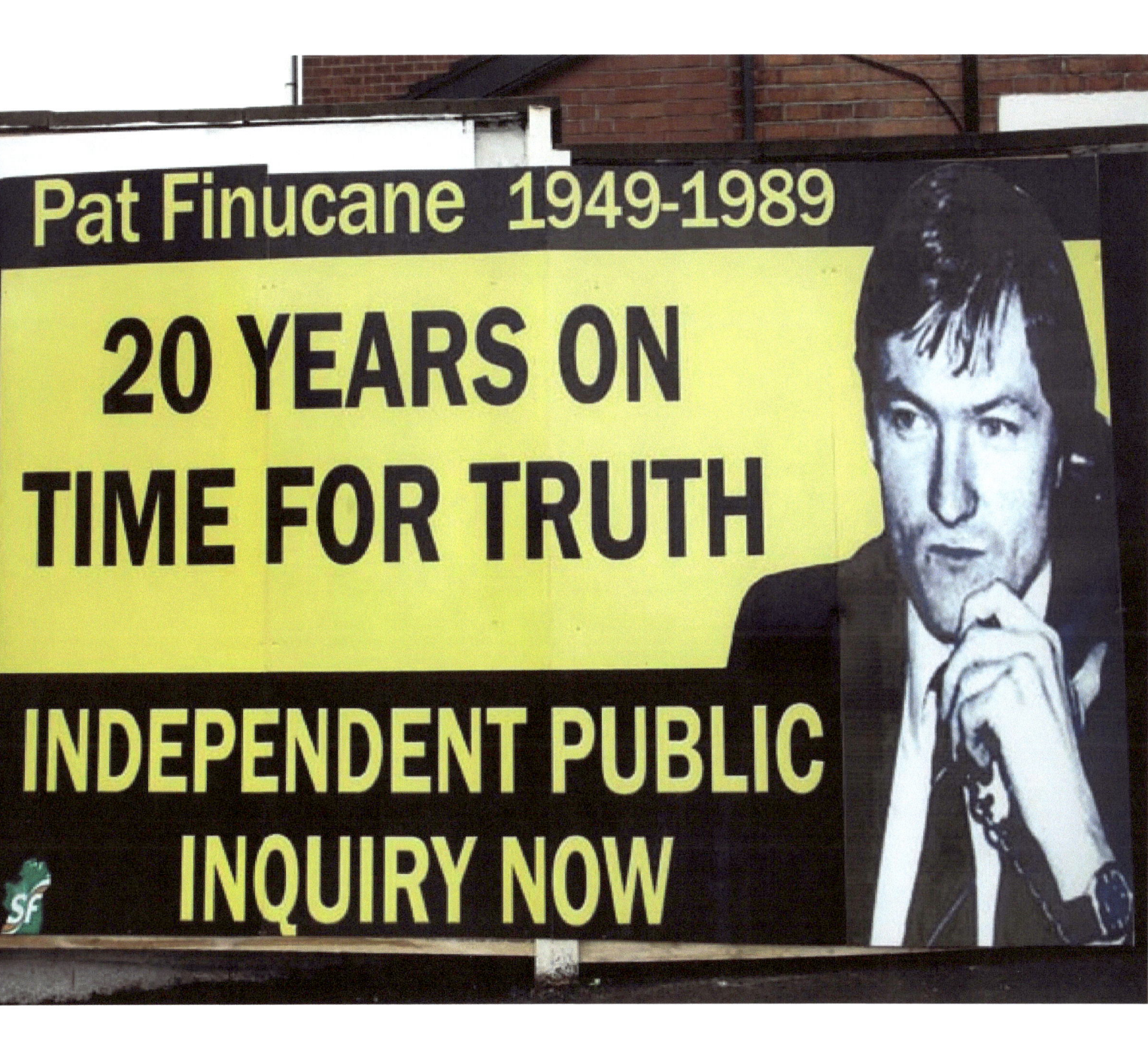

FREE PALESTINE NOW!

BOYCOTT ISRAELI GOODS!

IRISH PEOPLE SUPPORT GAZA

WANTED
FOR INTERNATIONAL TERRORISM

OPPRESSION **TORTURE** **MURDER** **BRUTALITY**

Ógra Shinn Féin

- This book has been produced by Kevin Traynor of Aisling Photography. For more information about Aisling Photography, why not contact us at www.aislingphotographyni.co.uk where more great Belfast images are available to look at and buy. Hope you enjoyed the book. Thanks.

This book features images from the following locations - Falls Road, Poleglass, Glen Road, Whiterock, Lenadoon, Clonard, Creggan, Derry, Newry, Andersontown, Ardoyne, Crossmaglen, Twinbrook, Short Strand, Springfield Road, Beechmount, Divis, Glencolin, Ormeau Road, Ballymurphy, Shaws Road, Armagh, Lurgan, St. James's and New Lodge.

www.ingramcontent.com/pod-product-compliance
Lightning Source LLC
Chambersburg PA
CBHW041124300426

44113CB00002B/52